Outer S

Ethan Smith

Other Books by Ethan Smith

Barnyard Origami

Ocean Origami

Garden Origami

Outer Space Origami

Fun Origami in Outer Space

Ethan Smith

Ethan Smith

Copyright © 2019 Ethan Smith

All rights reserved.

ISBN-13: 9781099942808

Introduction

Origami has been around for a long time. It is one of my favorite uses for paper. Origami started with only a few models. However, as time went on more models were designed and now there are hundreds of books teaching all kinds of different models. But it doesn't end there, more and more models are being designed every day. And now that math is becoming more advanced some people have tapped into that knowledge to make designing origami easier. Origami is still just as fun as it was when it was first invented, but now there are actual instructions that make folding origami easier, without difficult memorization. Although origami is very old, paper folding will always be fun.

Ethan Smith

About the Author

Ethan Smith has been home schooled his entire life. His love for origami started as a fun school project. By the time he was thirteen he had turned his passion for origami into online content and his website. He still enjoys paper folding, project designing, and otherwise expanding upon the art of origami.

Ethan Smith

Outer Space Origami

Table of Contents

Introduction v
About the Author vii
Symbols 1
Star 4
Moon 14
UFO 27
Comet 34
The Big Dipper 43
Rocket 53

Ethan Smith

Symbols

This symbol represents a crease that has been made.

This represents a valley fold that needs to be made.

This symbol represents a mountain fold that needs to be made.

Outer Space Origami

 This symbol represents the direction a valley fold or mountain fold needs to go.

This symbol means to fold a mountain fold then a valley fold, or the other way around.

 This symbol means to repeat the previous step on the other side of your model.

This symbol means to turn your model over.

 This symbol means to fold in one direction and then unfold it.

This symbol means to tuck in the part of your model that it is pointing towards.

Star

1. Fold the left edge of your model over to the right edge of your model. Crease well and unfold.

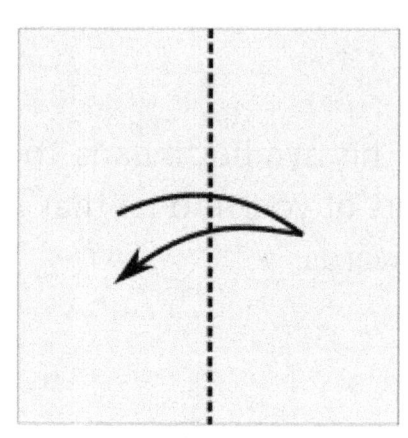

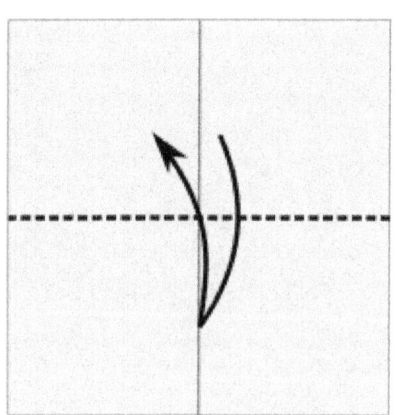

2. Fold the top edge of your model down to the bottom edge of your model. Crease well and unfold.

3. Turn your model over.

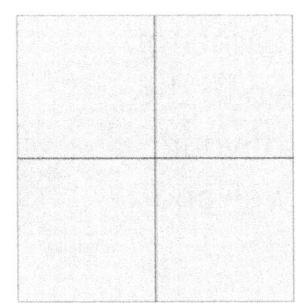 

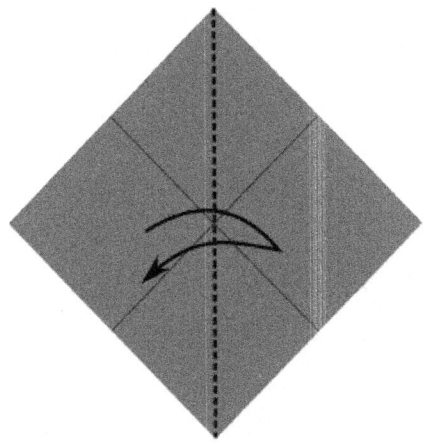

4. Fold the left corner of your model over to the right corner of your model. Crease well and unfold.

5. Fold the top corner of your model down to the bottom corner of your model. Crease well and unfold.

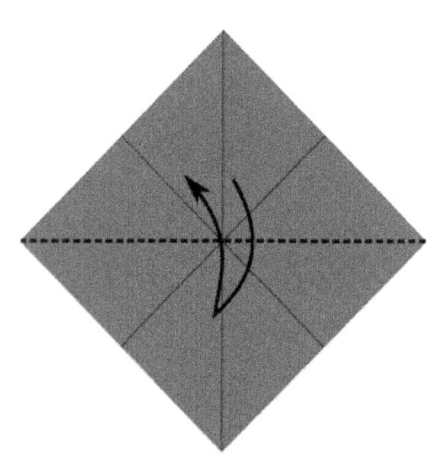

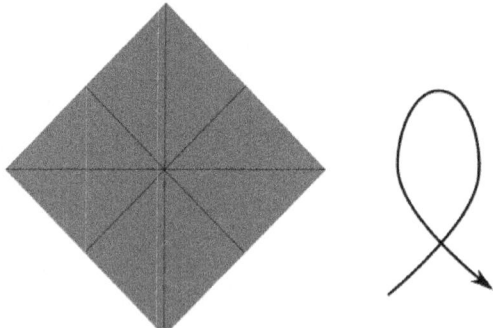

6. Turn your model over.

7. Fold the top and side corners of your model down to the bottom corner of your model.

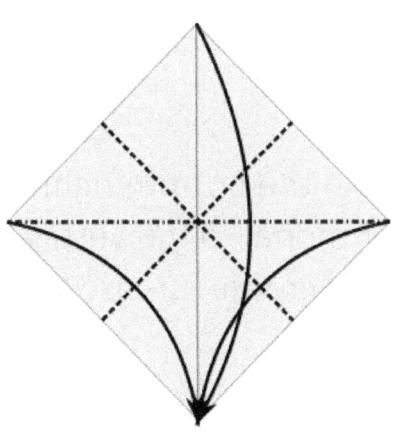

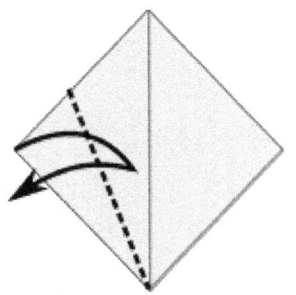

8. Fold the bottom left edge of your model to the vertical center crease. Crease well and unfold.

9. Fold the bottom right edge of your model to the vertical center crease. Crease well and unfold.

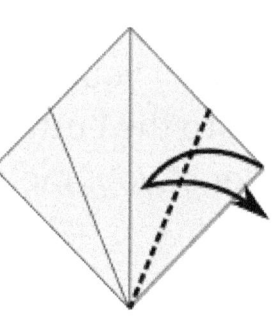

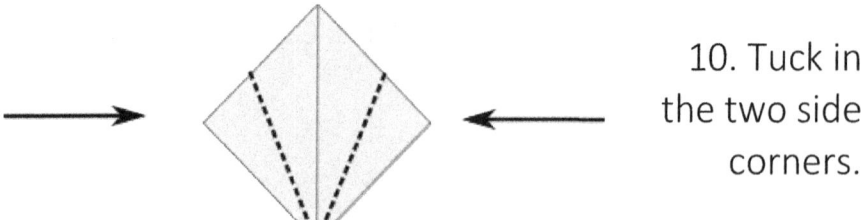

10. Tuck in the two side corners.

11. Fold the bottom corner of your model up.

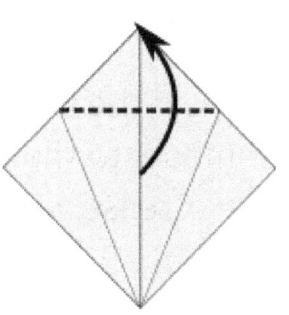

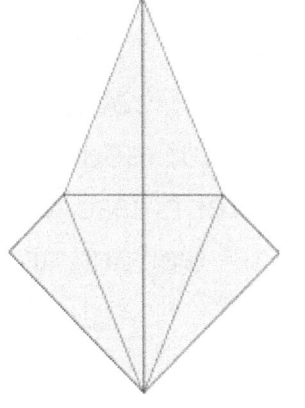

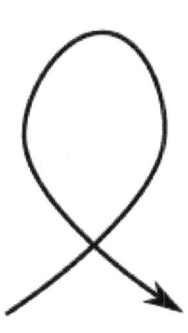

12. Turn your model over.

13. Fold the bottom left edge of your model to the vertical center crease. Crease well and unfold.

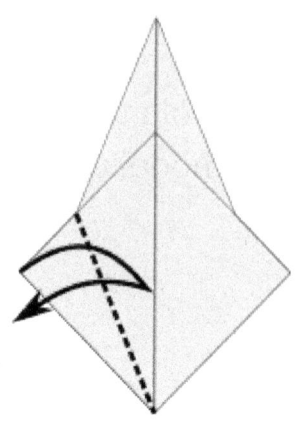

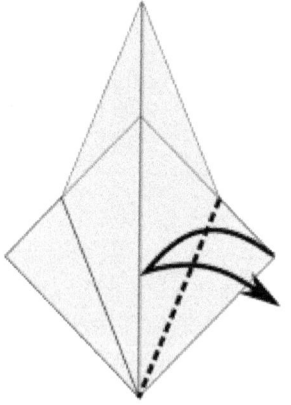

14. Fold the bottom right edge of your model to the vertical center crease. Crease well and unfold.

15. Tuck in the two side corners of your model.

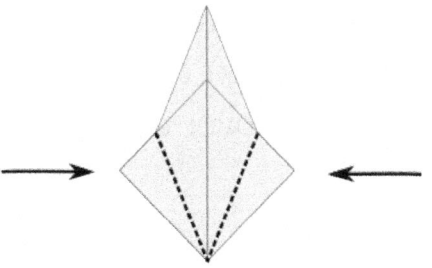

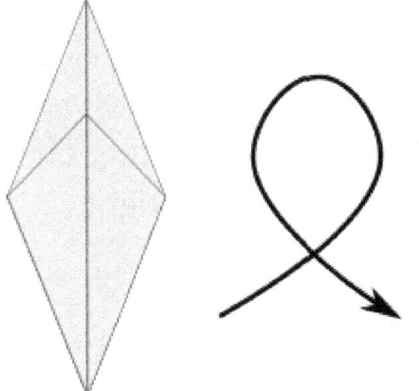

16. Turn your model over.

17. Open and squash fold the bottom left corner of your model over to the left.

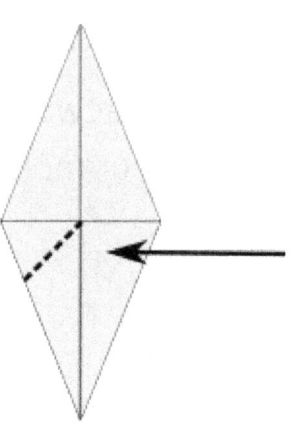

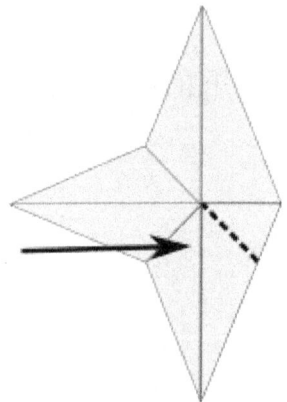

18. Open and squash fold the bottom right corner of your model over to the right.

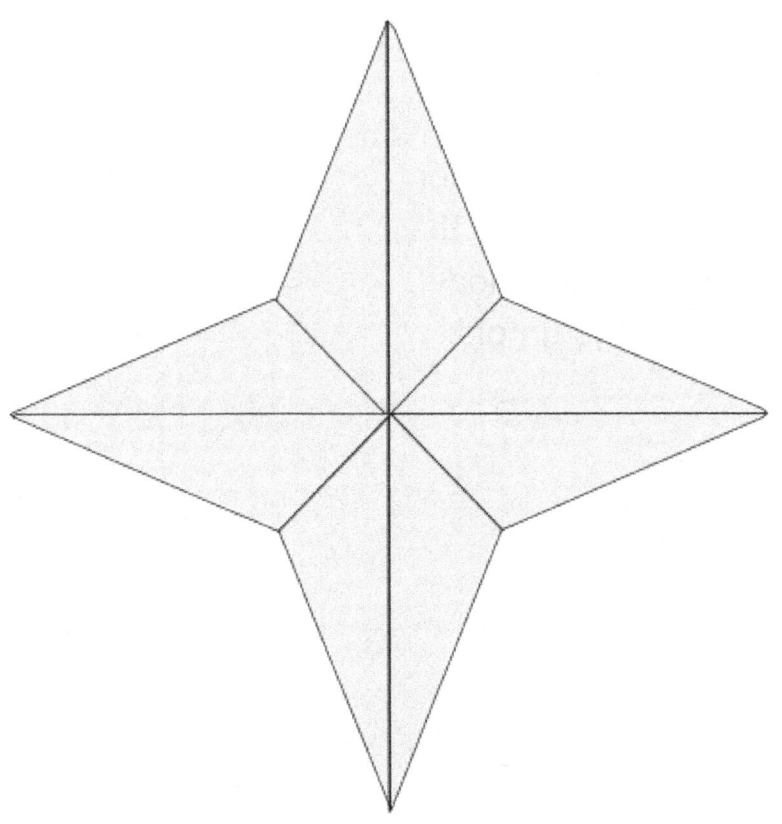

19. Your origami star is now finished.

Outer Space Origami

Moon

1. Fold the right corner of your model over to the left corner of your model. Crease well and unfold.

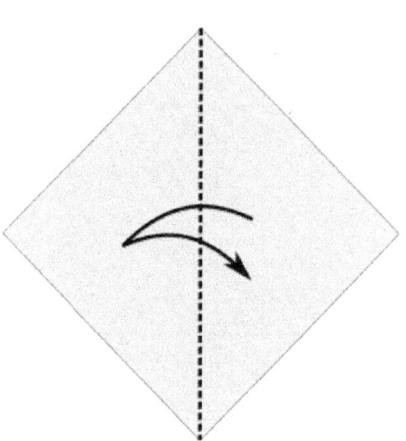

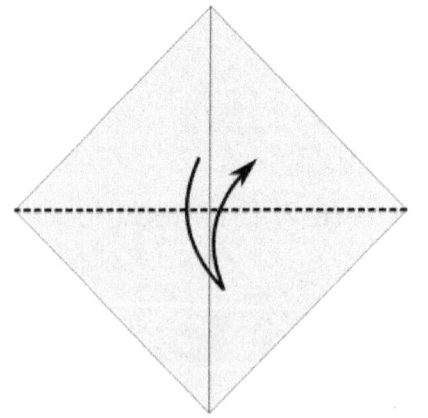

2. Fold the top corner of your model down to the bottom corner of your model. Crease well and unfold.

3. Fold the top right edge of your model over to the vertical center crease. Crease well and unfold.

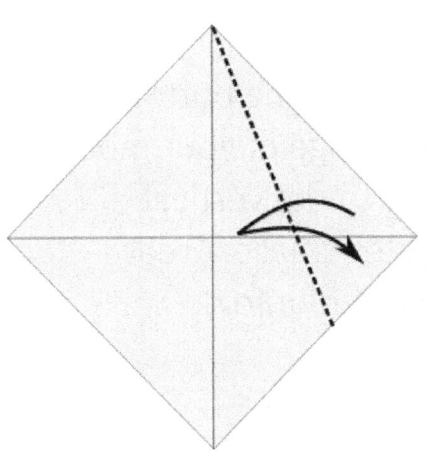

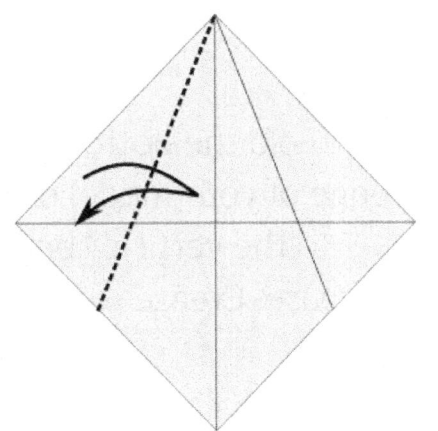

4. Fold the top left edge of your model over to the vertical center crease. Crease well and unfold.

Outer Space Origami

5. Fold the bottom right edge of your model over to the vertical center crease. Crease well and unfold.

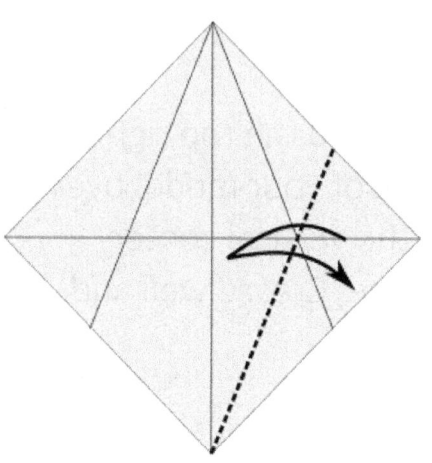

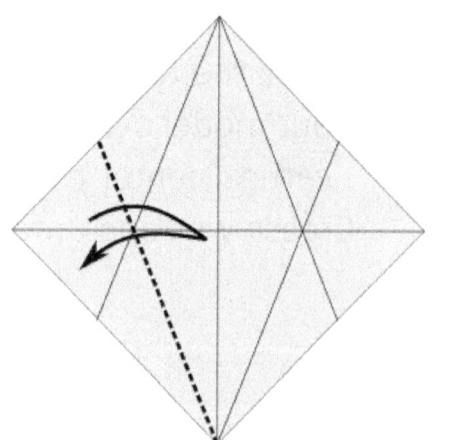

6. Fold the bottom left edge of your model over to the vertical center crease. Crease well and unfold.

7. Using all the folds made in the previous four steps, fold the edges of your model to the vertical center crease. Then fold the small triangle, that forms, up.

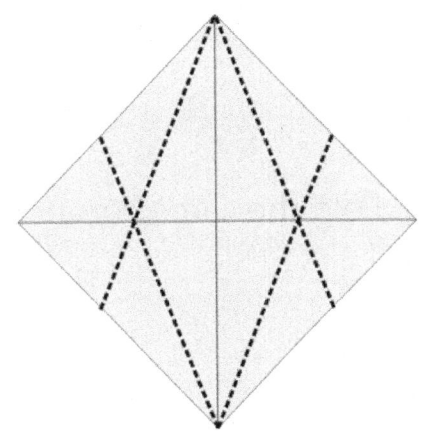

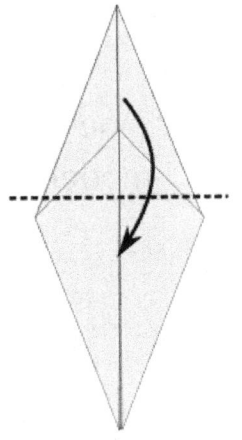

8. Fold the top corner of your model down.

Outer Space Origami

9. Fold the same corner back up.

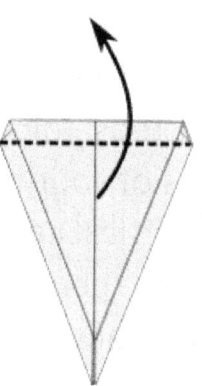

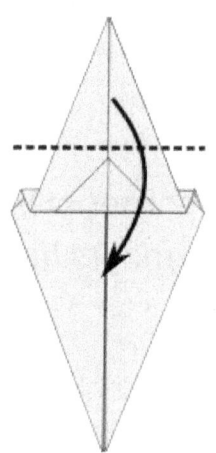

10. Fold the top corner of your model down.

11. Fold the same corner back up.

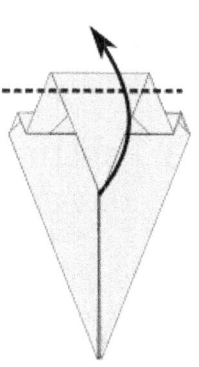

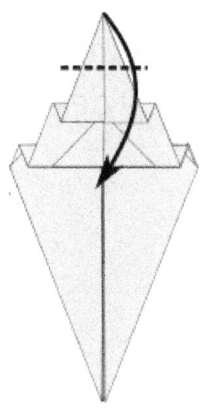

12. Fold the top corner of your model down.

Outer Space Origami

13. Fold the same corner back up.

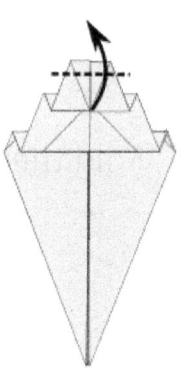

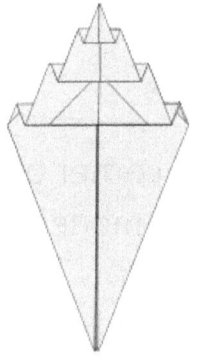

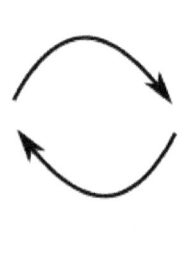

14. Rotate your model 180 degrees.

20

15. Fold the top corner of your model down.

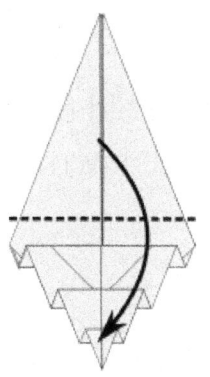

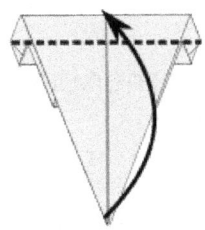

16. Fold the same corner back up.

17. Fold the top corner of your model down.

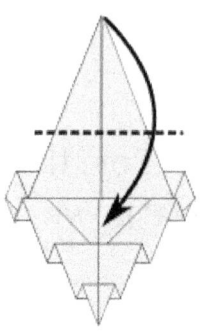

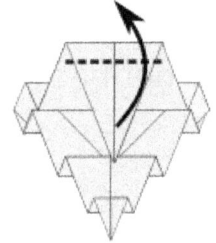

18. Fold the same corner back up.

19. Fold the top corner of your model down.

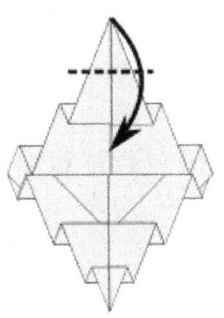

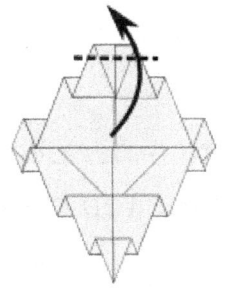

20. Fold the same corner back up.

21. Fold your model in half.

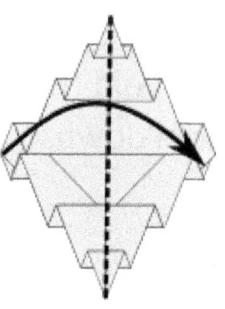

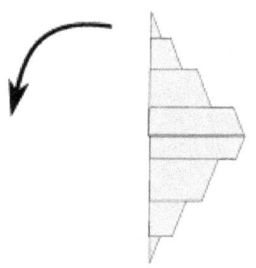

22. Pull the top corner over to the left, curving the top of right edge.

23. Pull the bottom corner of your model over to the left, curving the bottom right edge.

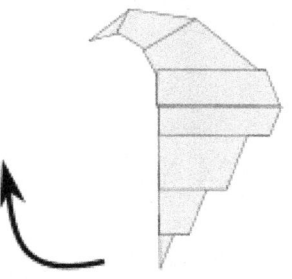

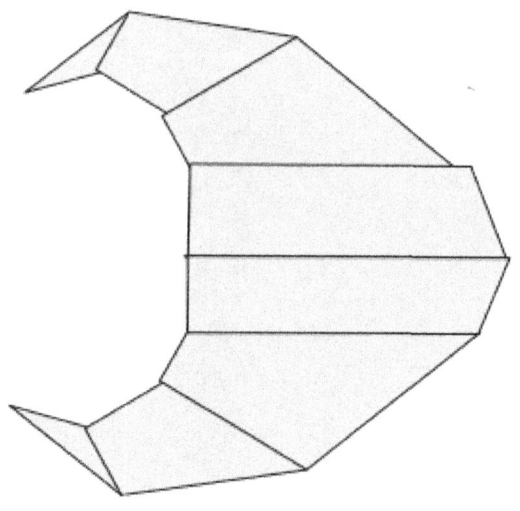

24. Your origami moon is now finished.

Ethan Smith

UFO

1. Fold the top corner of your model down.

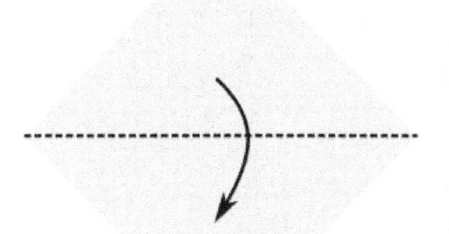

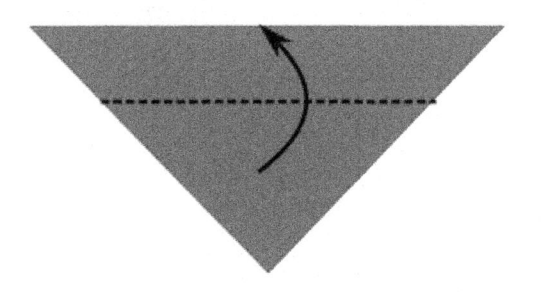

2. Fold the top layer of the bottom corner of your model up.

3. Fold the top corner of your model down.

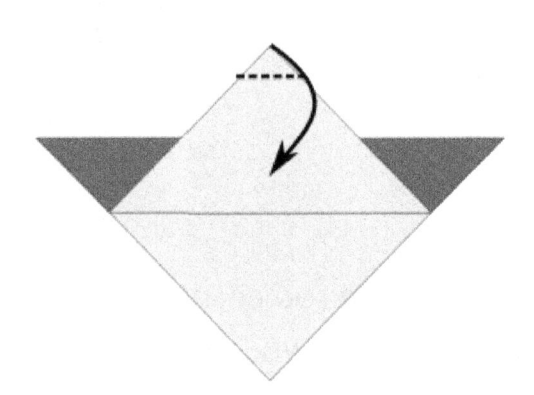

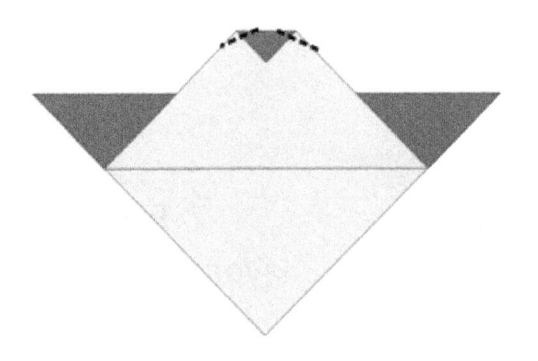

4. Fold the top side corners of your model inward.

5. Fold the bottom right edge of your model up to the horizontal crease.

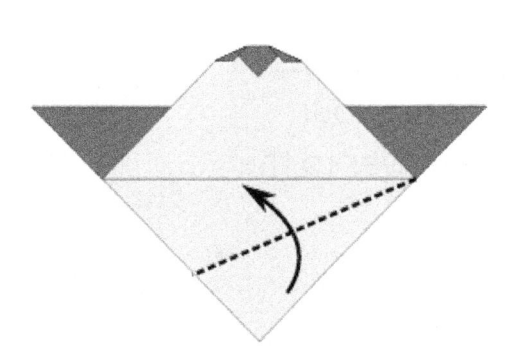

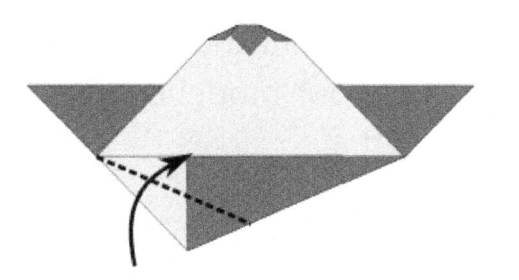

6. Fold the bottom left edge of your model up to the horizontal crease.

7. Fold the left corner of your model over to the right.

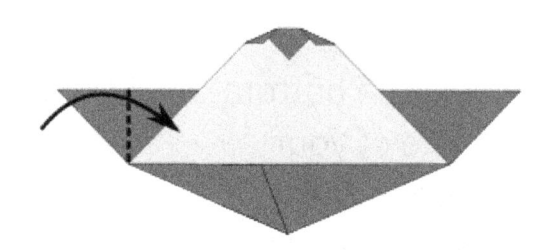

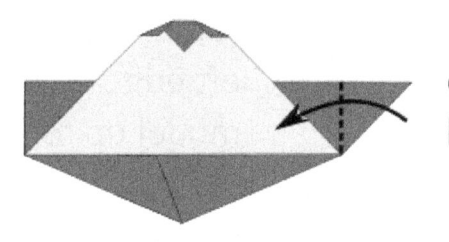

8. Fold the right corner of your model over to the left.

9. Fold the bottom left corner of your model up to the top horizontal edge.

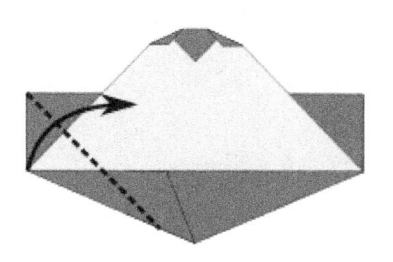

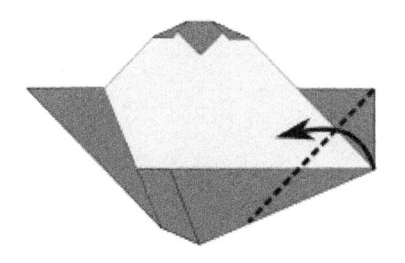

10. Fold the bottom right corner of your model up to the horizontal edge.

11. Turn your model over.

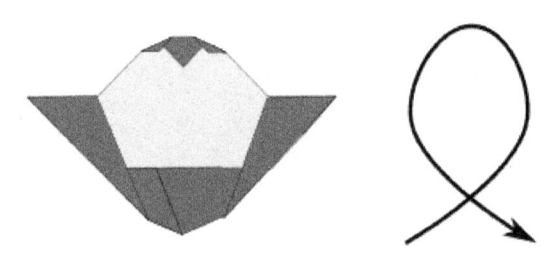

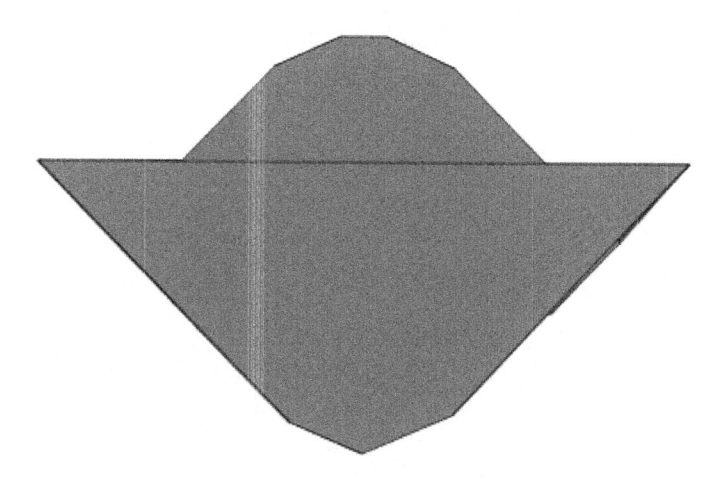

12. Your origami UFO is now finished.

Outer Space Origami

Comet

1. Fold the left edge of your model over to the right edge of your model. Crease well and unfold.

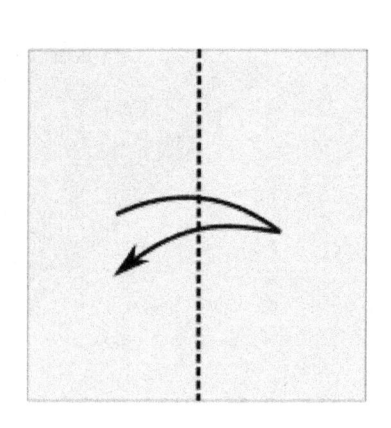

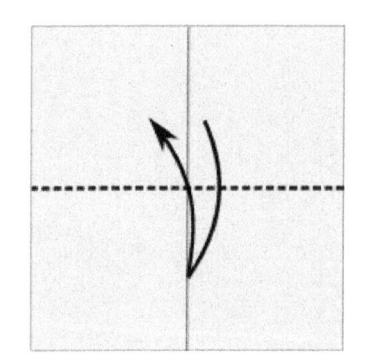

2. Fold the top edge of your model down to the bottom edge of your model. Crease well and unfold.

34

3. Turn your model over.

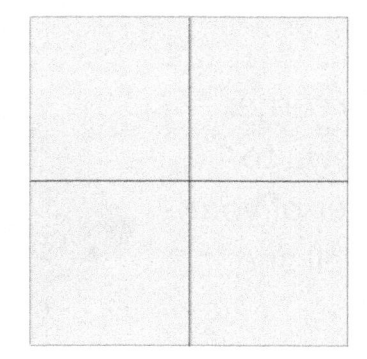

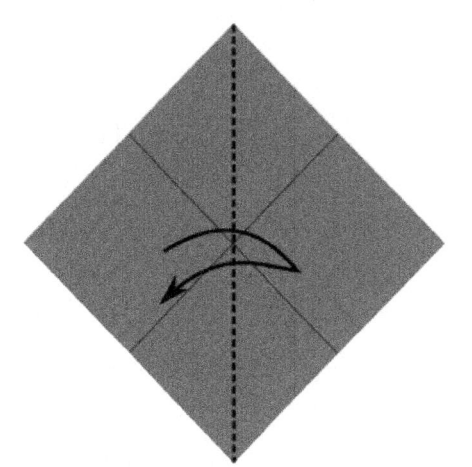

4. Fold the left corner of your model over to the right corner of your model. Crease well and unfold.

Outer Space Origami

5. Fold the top corner of your model down to the bottom corner of your model. Crease well and unfold.

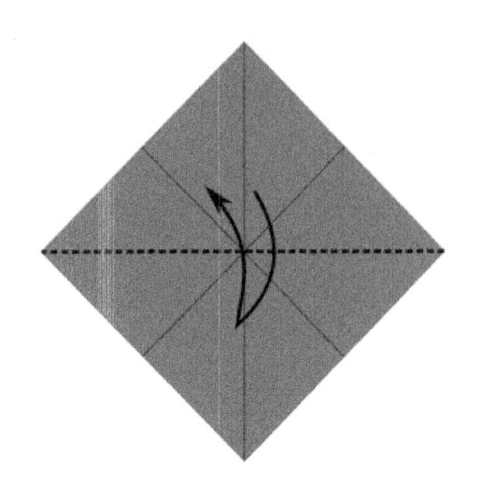

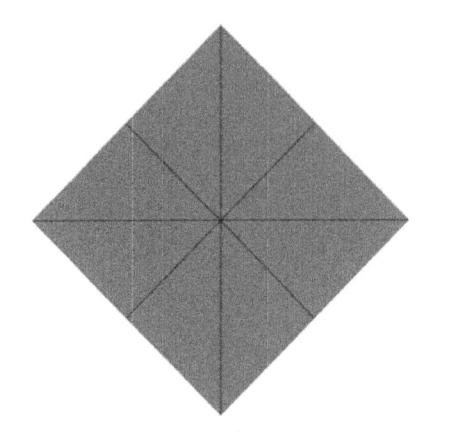

6. Turn your model over.

36

7. Fold the top and side corners of your model down to the bottom corner of your model.

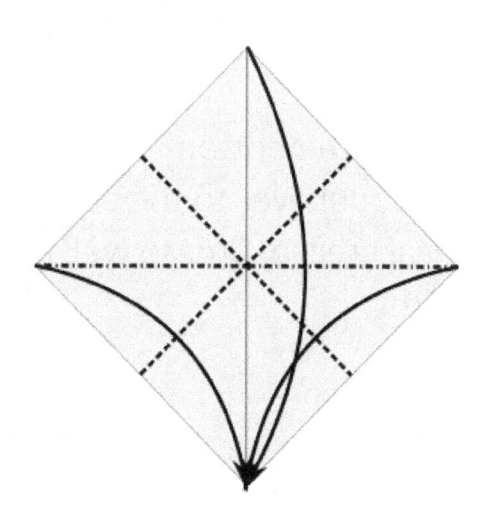

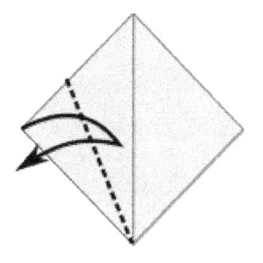

8. Fold the bottom left edge of your model over to the center vertical crease. Crease well and unfold.

9. Fold the bottom right edge of your model over to the center vertical crease. Crease well and unfold.

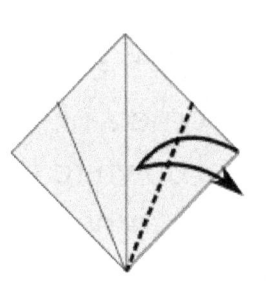

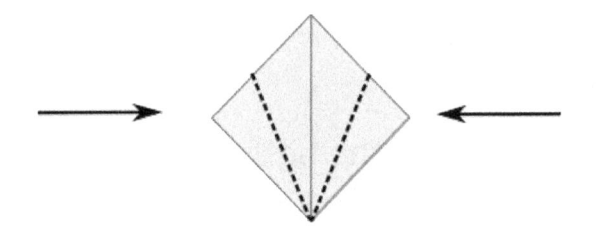

10. Tuck in the two side corners of your model.

11. Turn your model over.

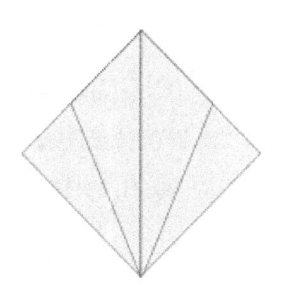

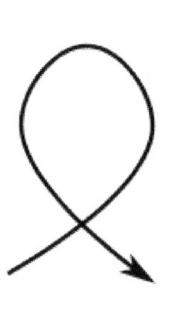

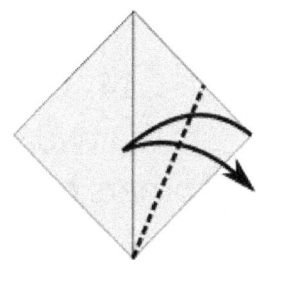

12. Fold the bottom right edge of your model over to the center vertical crease. Crease well and unfold.

13. Fold the bottom left edge of your model over to the center vertical crease. Crease well and unfold.

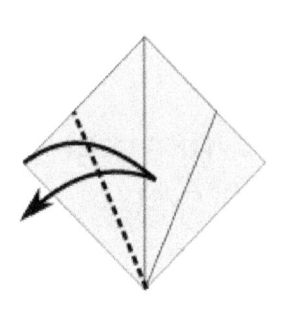

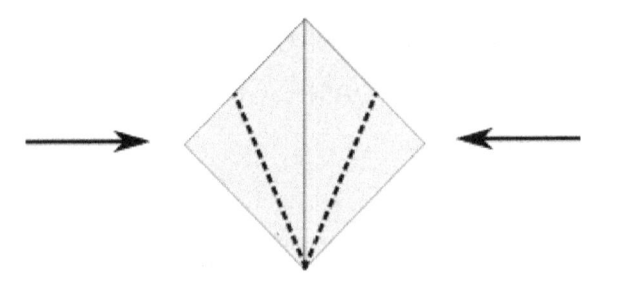

14. Tuck in the two side corners of your model.

15. Rotate your model 90 degrees.

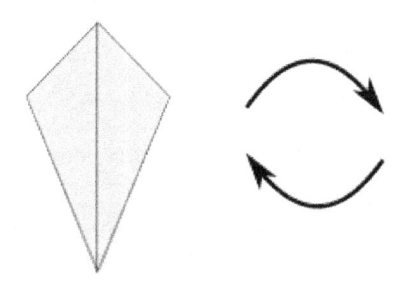

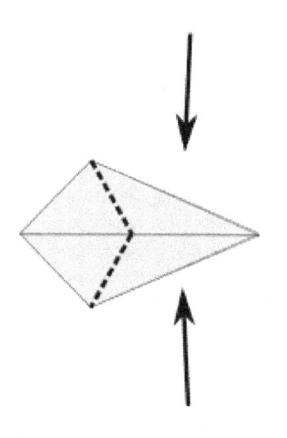

16. Pinch the right corner of your model to curve the tail of your model.

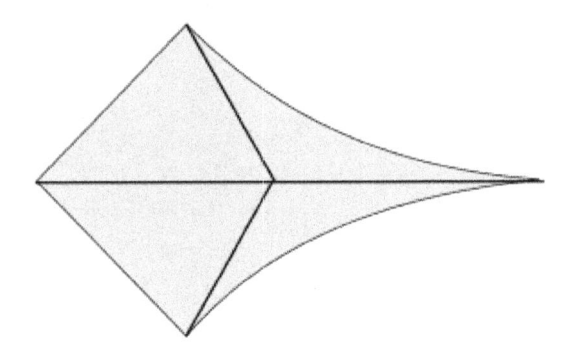

17. Your origami comet is now finished.

Ethan Smith

The Big Dipper

1. Fold the left corner of your model over to the right corner of your model. Crease well and unfold.

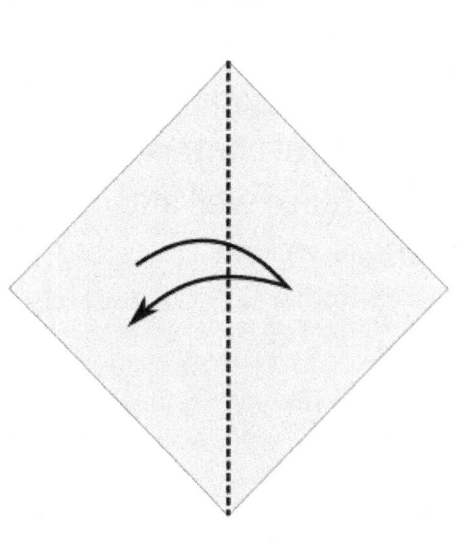

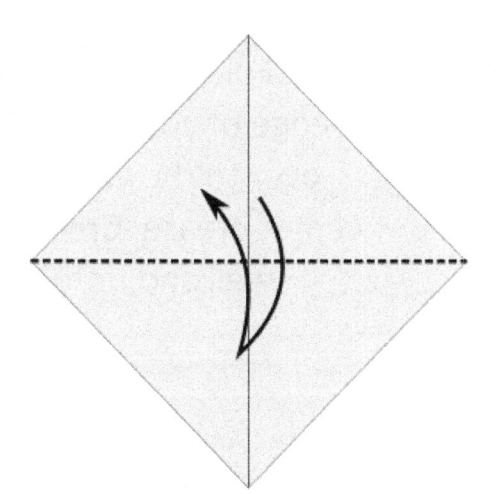

2. Fold the top corner of your model down to the bottom corner of your model. Crease well and unfold.

3. Fold the top right edge of your model over to the vertical center crease. Crease well and unfold.

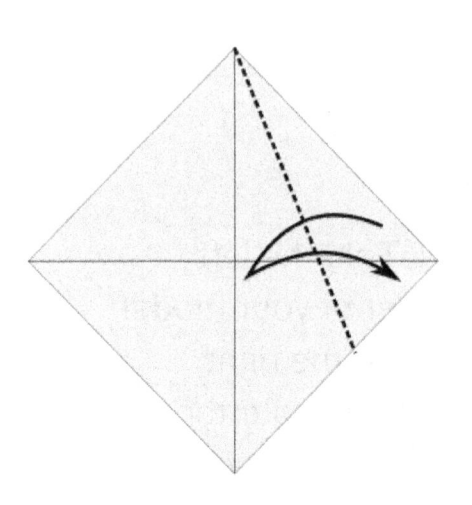

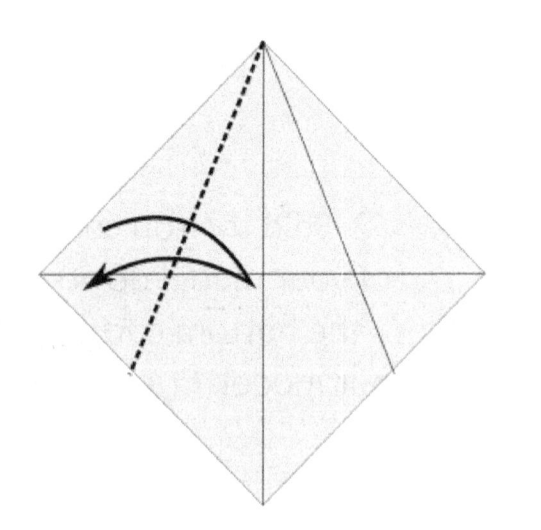

4. Fold the top left edge of your model over to the vertical center crease. Crease well and unfold.

5. Fold the bottom right edge of your model over to the vertical center crease. Crease well and unfold.

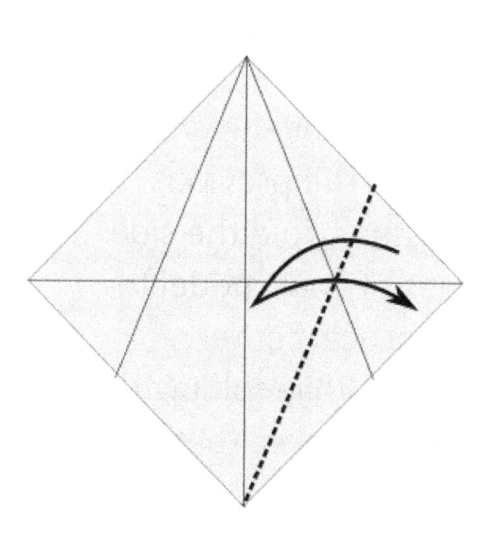

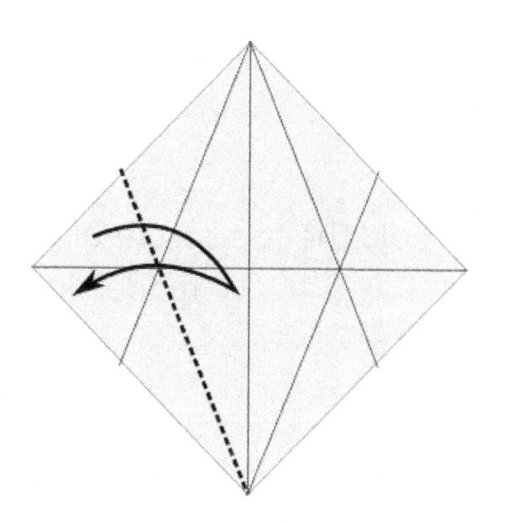

6. Fold the bottom left edge of your model over to the vertical center crease. Crease well and unfold.

7. Using all the creases made in the previous four steps, fold the side edges of your model to the vertical center crease. While folding the small triangles, that form, down.

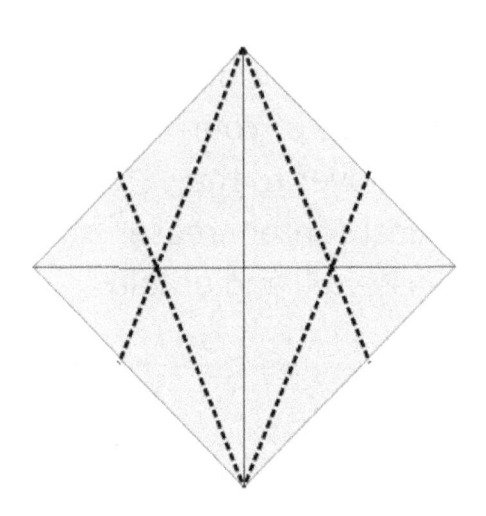

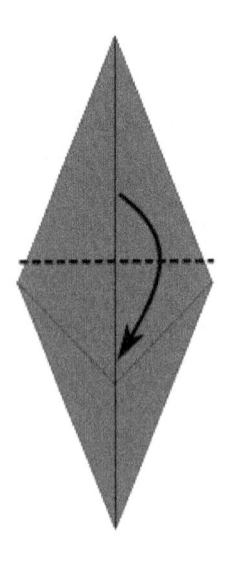

8. Fold the top corner of your model down.

9. Fold the same corner back up.

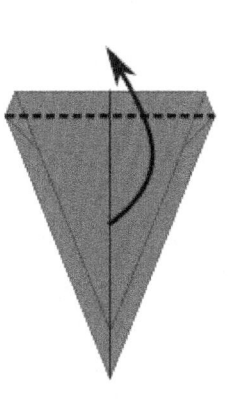

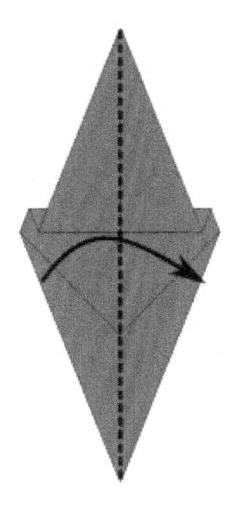

10. Fold your model in half.

Outer Space Origami

11. Rotate your model 90 degrees.

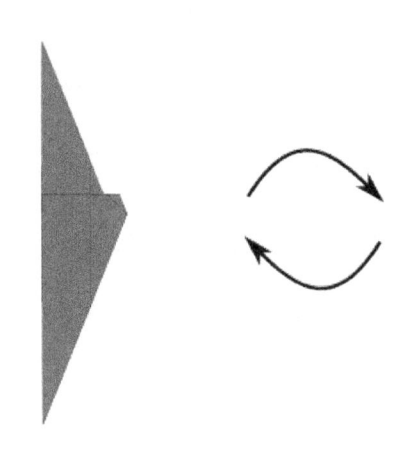

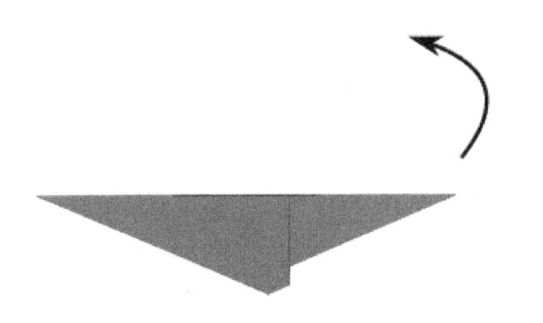

12. Pull the right corner of your model up.

13. Fold the left corner of your model up and over to the right.

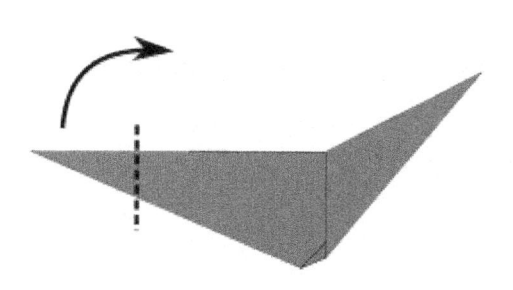

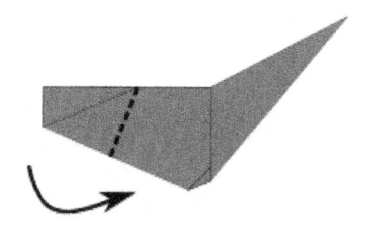

14. Fold the left edge of your model to the right underneath the rest of your model.

Outer Space Origami

15. Fold the bottom corner of your model underneath the rest of your model.

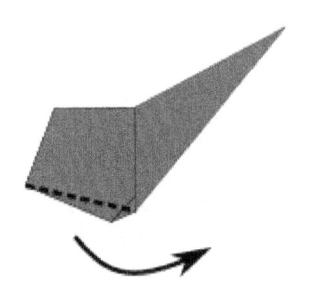

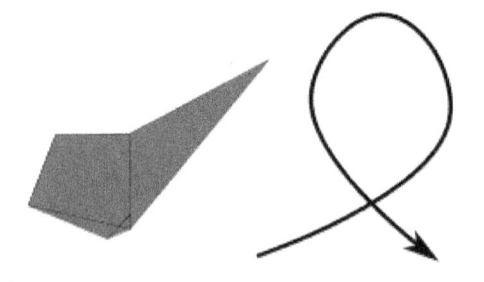

16. Turn your model over.

17. Fold the bottom corner of your model underneath the rest of your model.

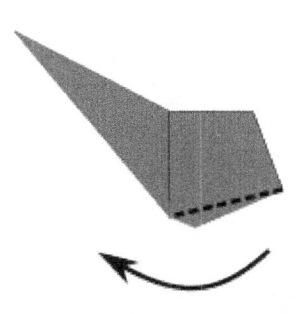

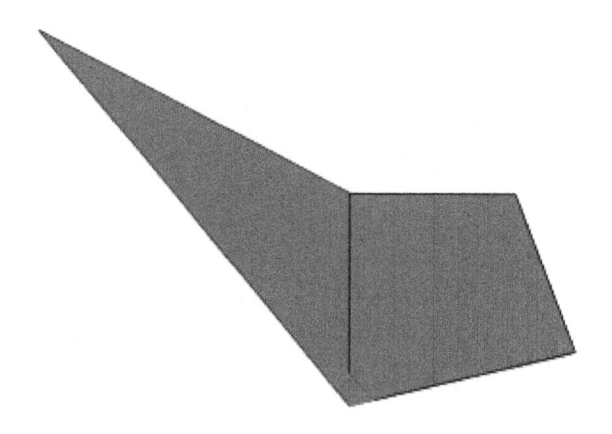

18. Your origami big dipper is now finished.

Ethan Smith

Rocket

1. Fold the left edge of your model over to the right edge of your model. Crease well and unfold.

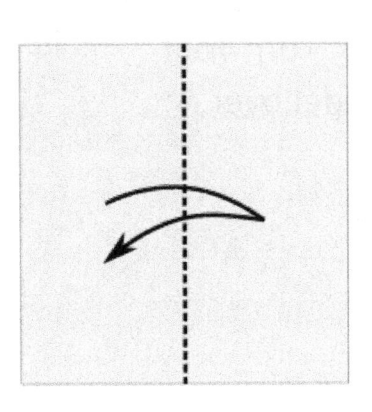

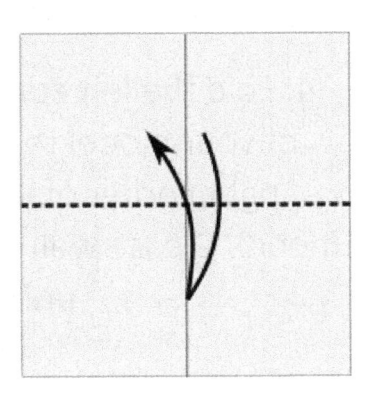

2. Fold the top edge of your model down to the bottom edge of your model. Crease well and unfold.

3. Turn your model over.

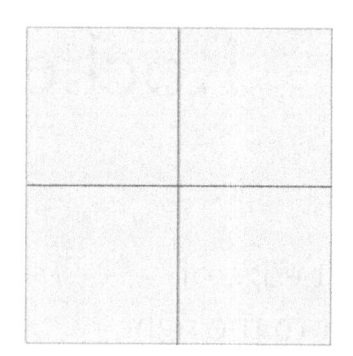

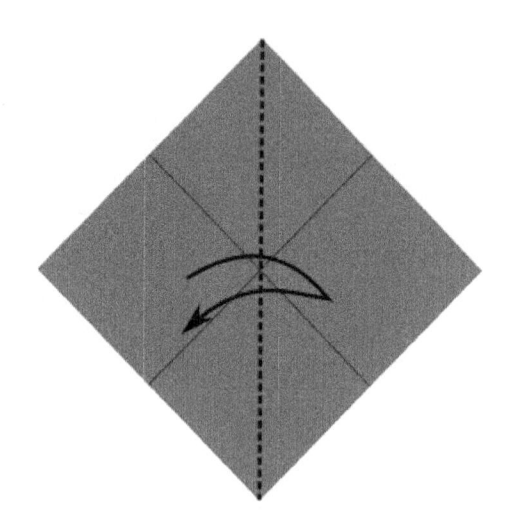

4. Fold the left corner of your model to the right corner of your model. Crease well and unfold.

5. Fold the top corner of your model down to the bottom corner of your model. Crease well and unfold.

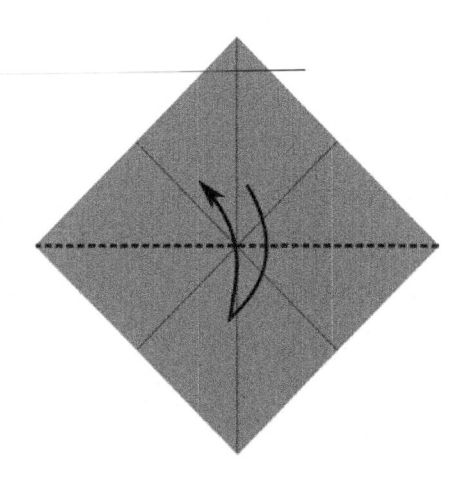

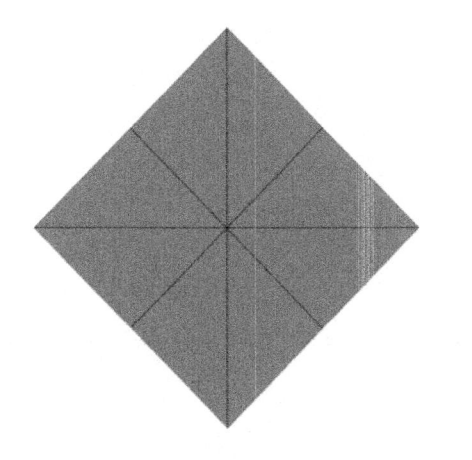

6. Turn your model over.

7. Fold the top and side corners of your model down to the bottom corner of your model.

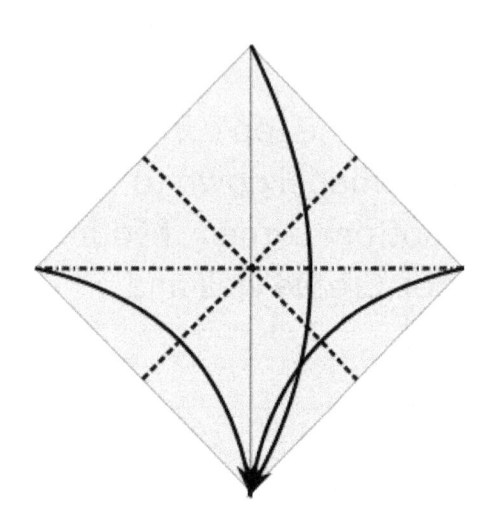

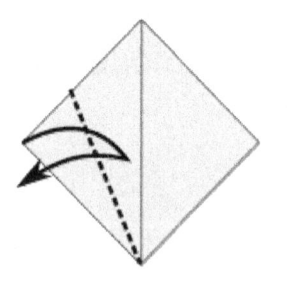

8. Fold the bottom left edge of your model to the center vertical crease. Crease well and unfold.

9. Fold the bottom right edge of your model to the center vertical crease. Crease well and unfold.

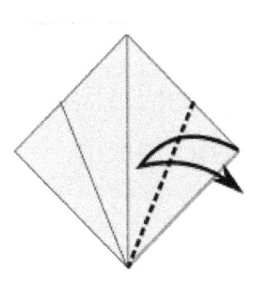

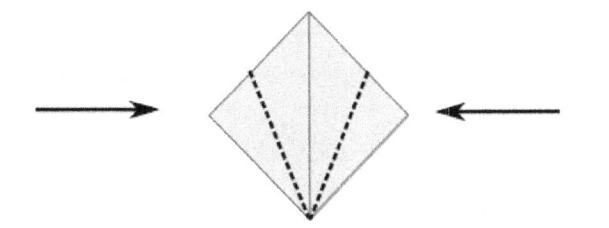

10. Tuck in the two side corners of your model.

11. Fold the bottom corner of your model up.

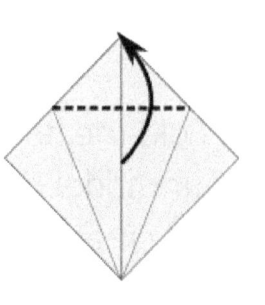

12. Turn your model over.

58

13. Fold the bottom left edge of your model to the center vertical crease. Crease well and unfold.

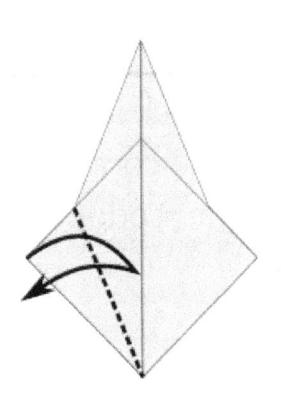

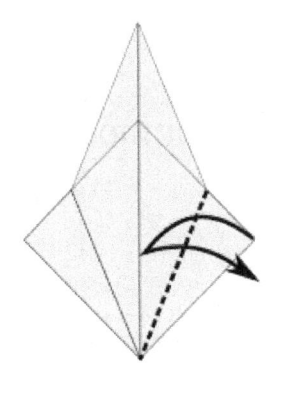

14. Fold the bottom right edge of your model to the vertical center crease. Crease well and unfold.

15. Tuck in the two side corners of your model.

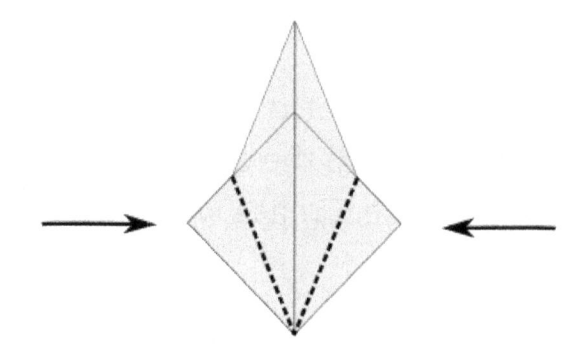

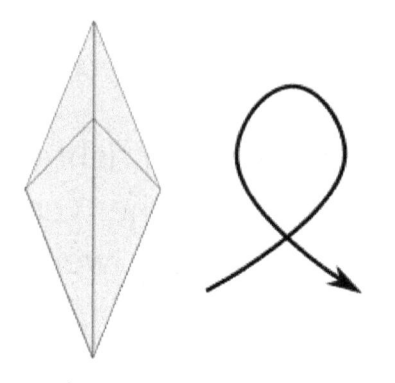

16. Turn your model over.

17. Fold the bottom right corner of your model up and over to the right.

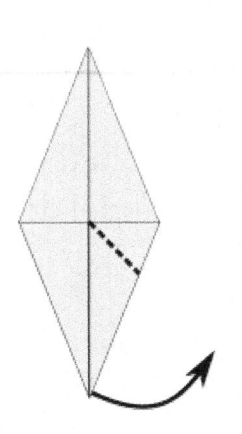

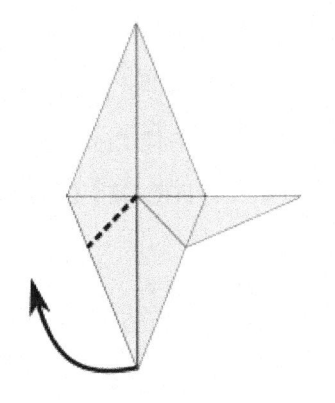

18. Fold the bottom left edge of your model up and over to the left.

19. Fold the left corner of your model down.

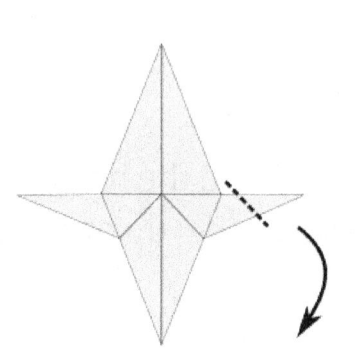

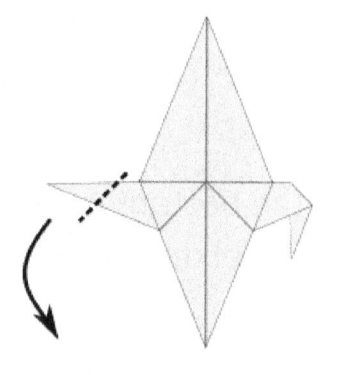

20. Fold the left corner of your model down.

21. Fold the bottom corner of your model up and then back down.

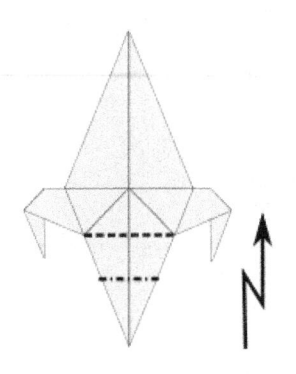

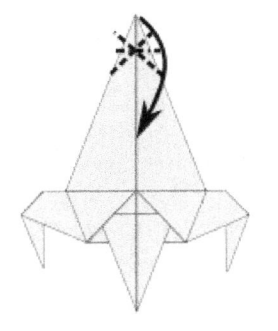

22. Fold the top corner of your model down and tuck in the sides of the diamond that forms.

23. Turn your model over.

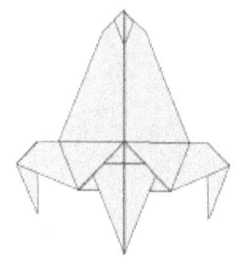

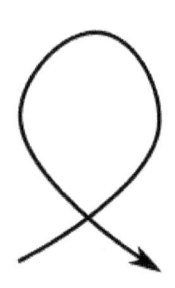

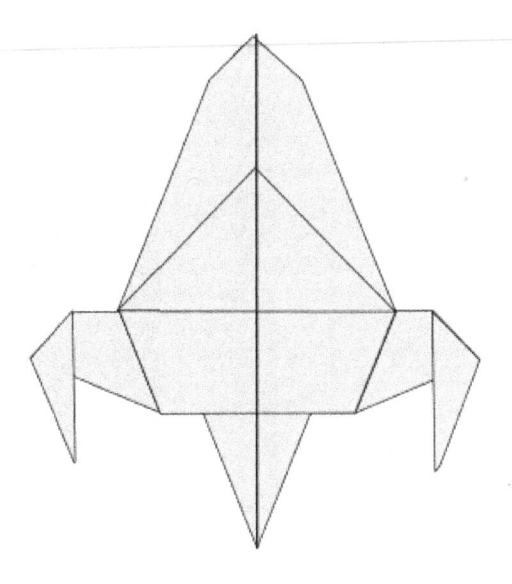

24. Your origami rocket is now finished.

Made in the USA
Columbia, SC
10 November 2022